# THE HISTORIC DESERTS OF IRAQ

## GEOGRAPHY HISTORY BOOKS
## CHILDREN'S ASIA BOOKS

Speedy Publishing LLC

40 E. Main St. #1156

Newark, DE 19711

www.speedypublishing.com

Copyright 2017

In this book, we're going to talk about the historic deserts of Iraq. So, let's get right to it!

The site of many ancient cultures and modern wars, Iraq is a desert country located in the Middle East. The Middle East straddles two different continents: Africa and Asia. Iraq is at the eastern edge of the Arab countries of the world.

Tabriz
Urfa
eppo
Mosul
Qazvin
SYRIA
Kirkuk
Te
ripoli
Qom
Euphrates
Tigris
Kermansha
Damascus
Baghdad
E
Amman
IRAQ
I
WEST BANK
a City
Basra
Ābādān
ORDAN
Sakākah
Kuwait City
KUWAIT
Pers
Tabūk
Man
Ad Dam

# WHERE IS THE COUNTRY OF IRAQ?

f you look at a world map, you will see that Iraq is in the same latitude as the southern part of the United States. It covers about 437,000 square kilometers, which is about the same size as the state of California.

The country of Iraq is bordered by six other Middle Eastern countries and is almost landlocked except for a small stretch of coastline along the Persian Gulf. Turkey is at its northernmost border. On its eastern border is the country of Iran. On its northwest border is the country of Syria and to its direct west is Jordan. On its southern border is the country of Saudi Arabia. The small country of Kuwait is wedged between Saudi Arabia and Iran on Iraq's southeast edge.

TURKEY
SYRIA
IRAQ
Mosul
Erbil
Kirkuk
Sulaymaniyah
IRAN
Samarra
BAGHDAD
Ar Rutba
Ramadi
Tigris
JORD.
Karbala
Kut
Najaf
Euphrates
Nasiriyah
SAUDI
ARABIA
Basra
Umm Qasr
Persian
Gulf
KUWAIT

THE FERTILE CRESCENT MAP

**T**he Tigris and Euphrates Rivers travel through Iraq and Iraq is in the eastern region of a larger piece of land that has been called "the fertile crescent."

EUPHRATES RIVER

The water in the rivers is fed by melting snow from the country's northern neighbor, Turkey. The river water creates fertile soil that supports farming, a major core of Iraq's economy along with its petroleum and natural gas reserves. However, despite this fertile area, for the most part, Iraq is largely a desert with an arid and semi-arid climate.

KURDISTAN REGION IN IRAQ

# THE FOUR LAND REGIONS OF IRAQ

raq has four distinctly different regions of land:

- The lower valley created by the Tigris and Euphrates Rivers

- The upper valley also created by the two rivers

- The mountains of the northeastern region

- The desert zone

# THE LOWER VALLEY

**T**his valley is a plain that drains very poorly. It begins north of the capital city of Baghdad and then extends in a south direction to the edge of the Persian Gulf. The southern part of the valley has large lakes that are shallow and a marshy area near the gulf. In ancient times, Babylonia was located in the lower valley.

CITY OF BAGHDAD

HASANKEYF VILLAGE

# THE UPPER VALLEY

The upper valley is actually composed of several valleys that are formed by the Tigris River and its branching rivers called tributaries. This region has grasslands and is higher in elevation with more hills than the terrain in the lower valley. In ancient times, the Assyrians lived there.

# THE MOUNTAINS

The mountains in the country's northeast region are an extension of Iran's Zagros Mountains. They are tall, craggy mountains that have 10,000-foot tall peaks.

ZARGOS MOUNTAINS

An ethnic population called the Kurds inhabits these mountains that stretch into several different countries.

THE ANCIENT VILLAGE IN ZAGROS MOUNTAINS

# THE DESERT ZONE

The land that lies west and also southwest of the River Euphrates is considered to be the desert zone of the country. This zone is composed of two major deserts, the Syrian and the Arabian.

These deserts are so vast that together they cover most of the Arabian Peninsula. They encompass sections of all the countries on the western borders of Iraq as well as Iraq itself.

ARABIAN DESERT

The desert zone is too harsh for most people, but the nomadic Bedouin people have lived on this rocky plain for thousands of years. Among the rocks, there are also a few stretches of sand.

An interesting geographic feature makes a pattern throughout the desert. These are wadis, which are natural channels springing from the Euphrates River.

WADI RUM DESERT

They are only filled with water during flooding season. Some of these wadis are very long, some are over 250 miles in length, and they are bone dry during most of the year.

The desert of western and southern Iraq covers a landmass of about 168,000 square kilometers or 64,900 square miles, which is about 40% of the country. The western part of the desert zone is part of the Syria Desert. Elevations there get to 1,600-foot heights. The southern desert is a part of the much larger Arabian desert.

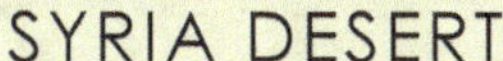


t is so vast that it is separated into two distinctly different regions, the Al-Hajarah to the west and the Al-Dibdibah to the east. The elevation in the desert to the south varies. The average peaks are from 1,000 feet to 2,700 feet in height.

DESERT OF JORDAN

The highest elevation is at a point where the border of Iraq meets up with the countries of Jordan and Saudi Arabia at Mount Jabal 'Unayzah, which is a 3,119-foot peak.

# AL-HAJARAH, TO THE WEST

The desert terrain in this region is very rocky with lots of ridges as well as depressions in the earth. It also has many wadis.

WADI AL-BATIN

# AL-DIBDIBAH, TO THE EAST

This portion of the desert is much more sandy than Al-Hajarah and has scrub plants. A very deep wadi, called Al-Batin, travels about 45 miles from a northeast to a southwest direction through this desert. Since the year 1913, it has been the boundary separating the western portion of Kuwait from Iraq.

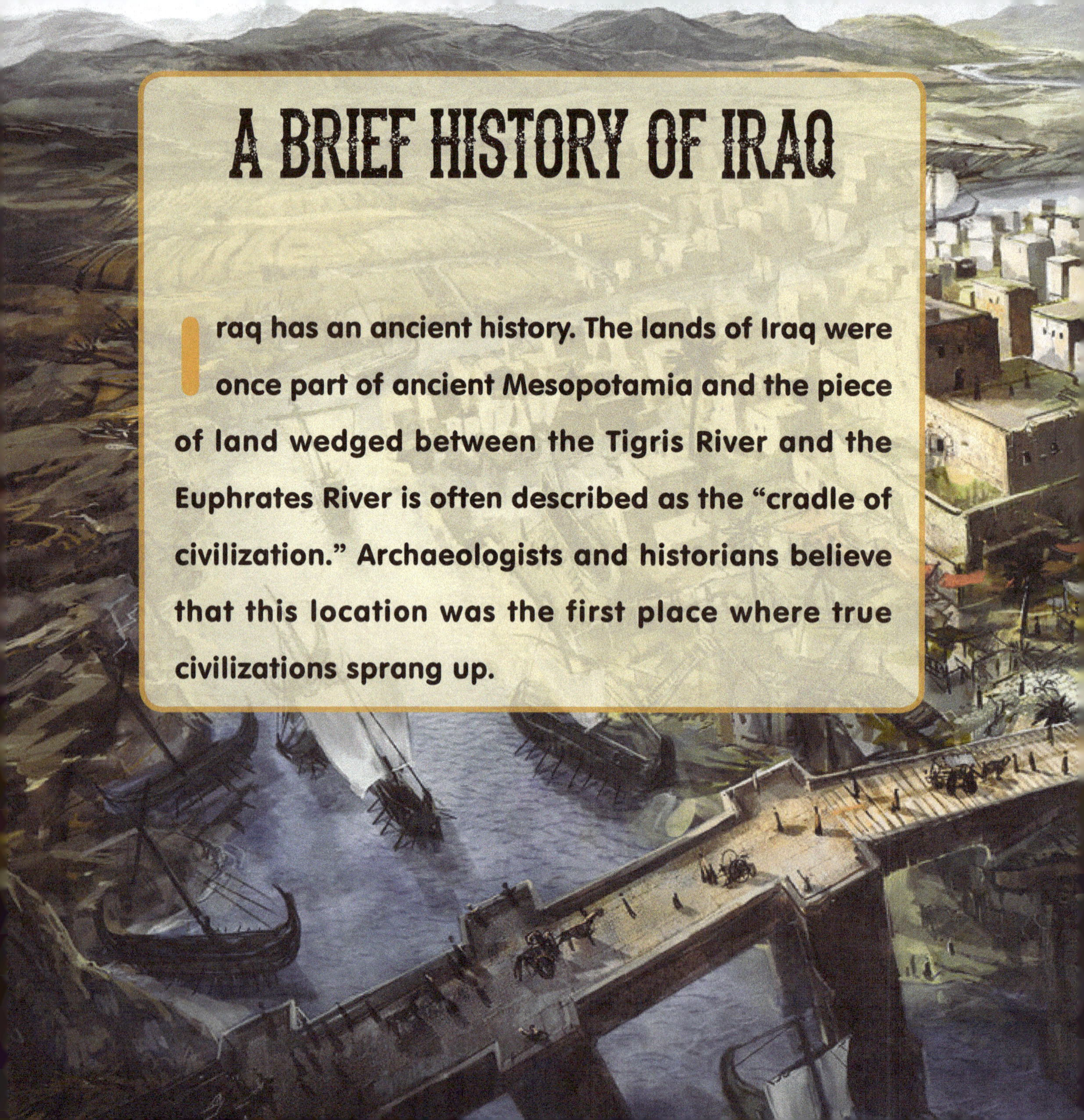

# A BRIEF HISTORY OF IRAQ

raq has an ancient history. The lands of Iraq were once part of ancient Mesopotamia and the piece of land wedged between the Tigris River and the Euphrates River is often described as the "cradle of civilization." Archaeologists and historians believe that this location was the first place where true civilizations sprang up.

ANCIENT MESOPOTAMIA

A round 3000 BC, the Sumerian people began the first civilization in what is now Iraq. The Sumerians were very advanced for their era. They created the first type of writing known on Earth called cuneiform. It was drawn with wedge-shaped symbols. Scribes wrote these symbols using blunt instruments on tablets of clay. The Sumerians thrived in the valley formed by the Tigris and Euphrates river system for more than 3,000 years.

CUNEIFORM

CODE OF HAMMURABI

After the Sumerians, the next great empire was that of the Babylonians. They began to rise to power around 1792 BC. Their king was named Hammurabi and he wrote the first codes of laws on Earth.

RESTORED RUINS OF ANCIENT BABYLON

The city of Babylon, which was located on the banks of the Euphrates, became the world's largest city inhabited by a population of over 200,000 at one time in history.

**E****ventually, the great Babylonian Empire was defeated around 539 BC by Cyrus the Great who led the Persians. Over the next few centuries the land was conquered many times by different kingdoms.**

CYRUS THE GREAT

At one point, Alexander the Great from Greece ruled. Then the Parthians, followed by the Romans, and once again the Persians all ruled in succession. The Muslims came into power in the 7th century AD and the Islamic Empire ruled for about 500 years.

OTTOMAN SOLDIERS

IRAQI T-72 TANKS
(PERSIAN GULF WAR)

**B**y 1958, Iraq was known as a republic, but, in truth, its system of government was a dictatorship. The last dictator in power in Iraq was Saddam Hussein. When the Iraqi troops invaded their southern neighbor Kuwait in 1990, it was the start of the Persian Gulf War.

raq was forced to retreat after the United States and other countries fought in Operation Desert Storm. The United Nations placed restrictions on Iraq in regard to the types of weapons it could possess or develop. However, Iraq, under the leadership of Saddam Hussein, refused to follow the agreements.

SADDAM HUSSEIN (1998)

n 2003, the United States joined forces with the United Kingdom to invade Iraq in what was called the Second Gulf War.

The reason was that Iraq had violated the United Nations measures and also because they were thought to have had weapons of mass destruction, such as nuclear bombs. The fighting was made more difficult due to the harsh desert environment. However, Baghdad fell and Suddam Hussein was captured.

Eventually he was executed for the crimes he committed. A new government was established in Iraq in 2010 and the following year the troops from the United States left. No weapons of mass destruction were found in Iraq.

A CEREMONY MARKING THE END
OF THE U.S. MISSION IN IRAQ

# SUMMARY

The country of Iraq is in the Middle East, which straddles two continents, Africa and Asia. It has four major geographic regions—two valley regions, a region of mountains, and an expansive desert. The Tigris and Euphrates river system has both an upper and lower valley.

The Zagros Mountains are situated at the northeast border. The desert is west and south of the Euphrates and is an extension of the Syrian and Arabian deserts. Iraq has an ancient history that goes back to the Sumerians in 3000 BC. It's been the site of modern wars fought within harsh desert conditions.

Now that you've read about the deserts of Iraq, you may want to read more about the largest deserts in the world in the Baby Professor book The Six Largest Deserts in the World! Geography Books for Kids 5-7.

Visit
BABY PROFESSOR
EDUCATION KIDS
www.BabyProfessorBooks.com
to download Free Baby Professor eBooks
and view our catalog of new and exciting
Children's Books